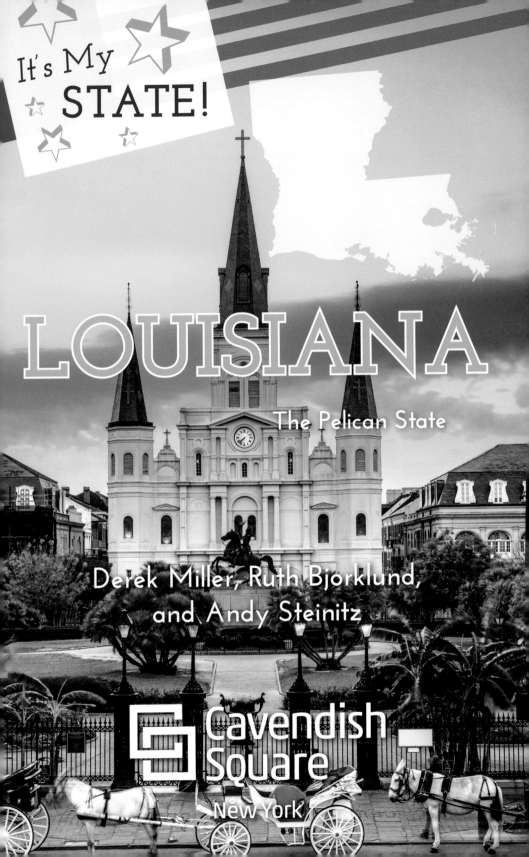

It's My
STATE!

LOUISIANA

The Pelican State

Derek Miller, Ruth Bjorklund,
and Andy Steinitz

Cavendish Square

New York

Published in 2019 by Cavendish Square Publishing, LLC
243 5th Avenue, Suite 136, New York, NY 10016

Library of Congress Cataloging-in-Publication Data

Names: Miller, Derek L., author. | Bjorklund, Ruth, author. | Steinitz, Andy, author.
Title: Louisiana / Derek Miller, Ruth Bjorklund, and Andy Steinitz.
Description: New York : Cavendish Square, 2019. | Series: It's my state! (fourth edition) |
Audience: Grades 3-5. | Includes bibliographical references and index.
Identifiers: LCCN 2017052583 (print) | LCCN 2017053558 (ebook) |
ISBN 9781502626271 (library bound) | ISBN 9781502626196 (ebook) |
ISBN 9781502644442 (pbk.)
Subjects: LCSH: Louisiana--Juvenile literature.
Classification: LCC F369.3 (ebook) | LCC F369.3 .M55 2019 (print) | DDC 976.3--dc23
LC record available at https://lccn.loc.gov/2017052583

Editorial Director: David McNamara
Editor: Caitlyn Miller
Copy Editor: Nathan Heidelberger
Associate Art Director: Alan Sliwinski
Designer: Jessica Nevins
Production Coordinator: Karol Szymczuk
Photo Research: J8 Media

It's My
STATE!

Table of Contents

SNAPSHOT
LOUISIANA

The Pelican State

Statehood

April 30, 1812

Population

4,684,333
(2017 census estimate)

Capital

Baton Rouge

State Flag

The state flag features the same image as the state seal: a bleeding white pelican feeding its three young. Underneath the pelican is a white banner with the words "Union," "Justice," and "Confidence." The flag's color is blue.

State Seal

In the center of Louisiana's state seal is a brown pelican— the state bird—on a blue background. It feeds three of its young by wounding itself. Around the pelican are the words "Union," "Justice," and "Confidence." A white ring around the outer edge contains the words "State of Louisiana."

State Song

Louisiana has two state songs. "Give Me Louisiana" by Doralice Fontane is a celebration of the state's natural beauty and heritage. Louisiana's other state song, "You Are My Sunshine," is famous across the United States. It was first performed by Jimmie Davis and Charles Mitchell as a country song. Jimmie Davis went on to be the governor of Louisiana.

HISTORICAL EVENTS TIMELINE

ca. 3500 BCE

Native Americans begin building complex earthen mounds in northern Louisiana.

1541

Hernando de Soto is the first European who is proven to have reached the Mississippi River.

1682

René-Robert Cavelier, sieur de La Salle travels down the Mississippi River to modern-day Louisiana and claims the region for France.

State Tree

Bald Cypress

In 1963, the bald cypress was designated Louisiana's state tree. It grows in swampy areas. Unlike most cypresses, it loses its leaves in the winter. This fact is the reason for its name. The bald cypress features distinctive knees that grow around its trunk. Knees are knobby pieces of wood that rise out of the ground (from the tree's roots). They anchor the tree in its swampy environment.

State Flower

Magnolia

The magnolia flower is Louisiana's state flower. This large, white flower grows on the southern magnolia tree, and the flower grows up to 12 inches (30 centimeters) across. Southern magnolias grow across the southeastern portion of the United States.

1803
France sells the Louisiana Territory to the United States in what is known as the Louisiana Purchase.

1812
Louisiana—a small part of the former Louisiana Territory—becomes the eighteenth state.

1838
The first Mardi Gras parade takes place.

State Crustacean
Crawfish

State Dog
Catahoula Leopard Dog

1975

The Superdome in New Orleans opens as the home of the Saints football team.

1988

New Orleans hosts the Republican National Convention.

2005

Hurricane Katrina devastates the city of New Orleans.

State Insect

Honeybee

State Cuisine

Gumbo

CURRENT EVENTS TIMELINE

2010
The New Orleans Saints win Super Bowl XLIV.

2015
John Bel Edwards is elected governor of Louisiana. He is the only Democratic governor in the Deep South.

2016
A historic flood hits southern Louisiana and does billions of dollars of damage.

Louisiana is known for its scenic bayous.

Geography

Louisiana's geography is a defining feature of the state. Its sleepy bayous and vast wetlands have captivated visitors and provided work for residents for centuries. In the past, pirates and communities of escaped slaves hid in the tangled marshes and isolated islands of the southern coast. Today, these areas are home to rare wildlife and beautiful parks.

A Diverse Landscape

The state of Louisiana is a boot-shaped area of land covering about 43,204 square miles (111,898 square kilometers). The state is divided into sixty-four parishes. These divisions are known as counties in most other states. The state capital, Baton Rouge, is in East Baton Rouge Parish. New Orleans, the largest city in Louisiana, is in Orleans Parish, in the southeastern part of the state.

One of the nation's most important rivers, the Mississippi River, meanders through the state. The Mississippi empties into the Gulf of Mexico, as do other rivers in Louisiana, such as the Atchafalaya, Ouachita, Sabine, Pearl, and Red Rivers. Many areas of Louisiana are low-lying

FAST FACT
Louisiana's location at the mouth of the Mississippi makes it an important shipping hub in the United States. Corn, wheat, and soybeans grown throughout the Midwest make their way down the Mississippi to Louisiana. From there, they are shipped around the world.

Louisiana borders Texas, Arkansas, and Mississippi.

wetlands, swamps, and marshes. However, the state also has rolling hills, forests, and grass prairies. The highest point in the state, Driskill Mountain, is located in northwestern Louisiana and rises 535 feet (163 meters). The lowest points are near the coast, where the land dips below sea level. Just off the coast, many islands protect the delicate inner shore. These islands are called barrier islands.

The view from Driskill Mountain, the highest point in Louisiana

The Gulf Coastal Plain

The entire state of Louisiana is part of a natural geographic region called the Gulf Coastal Plain. The Tunica Hills lie in a group of parishes known as the Florida Parishes in the eastern part of the state. Covered with flowering trees such as magnolia, sweetgum, dogwood, and hydrangea, the Tunica Hills also feature forests of beech, oak, and other hardwoods. Nearby West Feliciana Parish contains the wetlands and woodlands where the great naturalist John James Audubon studied and painted wildlife for his famous book *Birds of America*. While exploring the region, Audubon painted more than eighty birds, including the hooded merganser, pigeon hawk, white pelican, and blue heron, as well as the now-extinct passenger pigeon.

The Pearl River forms the state's southeastern border with Mississippi. The Pearl River splits into many channels and small, marshy, slow-moving waterways called bayous. These bayous and channels form large swamps and marshlands where trees are draped with Spanish moss. Honey Island Swamp, near Slidell, is the largest in the area. There, bald eagles, alligators, egrets, and wild turkeys roam among the oaks, cypresses, and water lilies. More than 50 square miles (130 sq km) of pristine wetland are filled with wild creatures and plants.

The Mississippi floodplain is an area of fertile land that lies along the banks of the famous river that winds through the state. The major cities of New Orleans and Baton Rouge are found in the floodplain. Over time, the river has reshaped the surrounding landscape. Levees, or ridges 10 to 15 feet (3 to 5 m) high, stop the river from flooding nearby areas. Some levees have formed naturally as sediment—rocks, dirt, sand, and other material—is pushed up onto land by the river as it flows or floods. People also build levees or strengthen natural levees with sediment or concrete. Beyond the levee walls, the land is very flat and filled with ponds, swamps, and bayous. Slight changes in ground level cause these areas to collect rain and floodwater.

The southern end of the Mississippi River opens into a **delta**. The river delta is a system of slow-moving channels of water and rich, muddy soil. There, the Mississippi drops about 500 million tons (453 million metric tons) of soil every year. When the mud blocks a channel, the water pushes through to form a new route.

The entire coast west of the delta into Texas is an **estuary**, where the freshwater of the Mississippi River and its offshoots meets the salty water of the Gulf of Mexico. The largest wilderness swamp in the nation, the Atchafalaya Basin, was created by all this water. Hundreds of species of birds stop there during their migrations. Fish fill its swamps, and reptiles and amphibians live in its tall cordgrass. The swamps are also home to notable species, such as the Louisiana black bear, pallid sturgeon, and American alligator.

The southwestern part of the state has many remarkable landforms, such as barrier islands, marshes, grasslands, beaches, and cheniers—oak-covered islands formed from crushed shells and sand. Rare and endangered creatures, such as the piping plover and the Kemp's Ridley sea turtle, find refuge along these coastal areas. Herons, egrets, pelicans, eagles, and a host of other shorebirds are also found along the Louisiana coast. Going north, a traveler will pass through the Cajun Prairie, where once-treeless grasslands have been replaced by thousands of acres of rice fields and pastures. This farmland gives way to rolling hills dotted with pine trees. These hills stretch toward the northwest border of the state.

Atchafalaya Basin is the country's biggest wilderness swamp.

Cameron Prairie National Wildlife Refuge

This alligator was photographed outside New Orleans.

Louisiana's Biggest Cities

(Population numbers are from the US Census Bureau's 2017 projections for incorporated cities.)

New Orleans

Baton Rouge

1. New Orleans: population 393,292

New Orleans is known as one of the most interesting cities in the world. Because of its history, the city's food, music, and dance are influenced by Caribbean, European, and African culture.

2. Baton Rouge: population 225,374

Baton Rouge is the farthest inland deepwater port on the Mississippi River. Therefore, it sees a lot of commercial and industrial activity. The city also boasts four colleges.

3. Shreveport: population 192,036

Located in western Louisiana near the Texas border, Shreveport is known for its riverboat casinos on the Red River. The city also offers parks, waterfront dining, shopping, and entertainment.

4. Lafayette: population 126,848

Lafayette is the center of Cajun culture in Louisiana and the United States. Food markets, concerts, and street festivals are just some of the activities that people enjoy there.

5. Lake Charles: population 77,117

Nicknamed "The Festival Capital of Louisiana," Lake Charles hosts more than seventy-five festivals each year. Contraband Days, the Louisiana Pirate Festival, is especially popular.

6. Bossier City: population 68,554

Bossier City is located across the Red River from Shreveport. Therefore, it shares the riverboat casinos with its neighbor. Bossier City also has a horse racetrack, parks, dining, and outlet shopping.

7. Kenner: population 67,451

Kenner is a suburb of New Orleans, located northwest of the city. Among Kenner's attractions is Rivertown, a historic district located on the city's original main street. It features shops, museums, theaters, and restaurants.

8. Monroe: population 48,371

Monroe is home to the Louisiana Purchase Gardens and Zoo, which features more than four hundred animals. The city also has several museums, including the Northeast Louisiana Children's Museum and the Biedenharn Museum and Gardens.

Shreveport

9. Alexandria: population 47,334

Alexandria sits in the center of Louisiana. The city has become a popular place to raise a family. *National Geographic Traveler* ranked it as one of America's top-ten "wilderness towns" because of the nearby national forests.

Lafayette

10. Houma: population 33,278

Houma was named after the historic Houma Native American tribe that lived, and continues to live, there. The Houma area has around 2,500 square miles (6,475 sq km) of swamps and wetlands, which are popular places to tour and go fishing.

Visiting City Park in New Orleans

City Park is a major attraction in New Orleans. It was founded in 1854 and covers 1,300 acres (526 hectares) of the city. The park is packed with fun and entertainment for the whole family.

The Carousel Gardens Amusement Park sits at the south end of City Park. It has all the rides of a carnival, from a tilt-a-whirl to a Ferris wheel. But its main attraction is the historic carousel. It is one of the oldest in the United States, and visitors can still ride on it today.

The New Orleans Museum of Art is also in the park. First opened in 1911, it is one of the largest art museums in the region. More than forty thousand objects are displayed there, including historic paintings indoors and sculptures in a large outdoor garden.

The Peristyle in City Park was built in 1907. Today, special events are held there.

Visitors can go in the museum and amusement park or just wander around the natural scenery. Footpaths wind their way around the park, and bridges cross the many lakes and bayous. Massive trees grow in the park, including eight-hundred-year-old live oaks! There is something for everyone to see in the historic and beautiful City Park.

Climate

Louisiana's warm temperatures and steady rains make the state a year-round paradise for gardeners. But Louisianans must also deal with tornadoes, hurricanes, other wind and rain storms, and often extremely high **humidity**.

Summers in Louisiana are long and hot. Winters are short and mild. In the northern city of Shreveport, the temperature typically stays above 90 degrees Fahrenheit (32 degrees Celsius) for most of the summer. The high humidity makes northern Louisiana steamy and uncomfortable in summer. During northern Louisiana's coolest month, January, temperatures are about 46°F (8°C). Record-setting temperatures in the state have occurred in the north. On August 10, 1936, the temperature in Plain Dealing reached 114°F (46°C). Minden recorded the coldest temperature, –16°F (–27°C), back in February 1899.

The Gulf of Mexico creates a steadier climate for southern Louisiana. The Gulf affects the winds and the air temperature, resulting in fewer extremes of hot and cold. Breezes from the Gulf cool off the land in summer and warm it in winter. Summer temperatures in southern Louisiana average 84°F (29°C). The winter temperatures average about 55°F (13°C).

Wind and rain affect the entire state. Northern Louisiana is in the path of strong winds that blow across the Great Plains and is on the southern edge of a region known as "Tornado Alley." Spring is the most threatening time of year for thunderstorms, hailstorms, and tornadoes, as cold air from the Great Plains runs into warm air from the Gulf of Mexico. When the weather fronts collide, air begins to swirl, forming funnel clouds and hail. Summer brings unstable weather to southern Louisiana. Violent hurricanes batter the coast with raging winds, high surf, flooding, and heavy rain.

The aftermath of a January 2017 tornado in Bossier Parish

Hurricane Ike made landfall in 2008.

FAST FACT

Most of New Orleans is below sea level. It is dry land only because of a system of levees that keep the water out. As a result, the city is vulnerable to storm surges— rising water that result from storms.

The Louisiana Purchase

The Mississippi River flows north to south, from Minnesota to Louisiana.

Since its founding in 1718, New Orleans has been a key city in North America. At that time, New Orleans controlled access to the Mississippi River—the main means of transportation for a large slice of the continent.

At the beginning of the 1800s, the fate of transportation along the Mississippi River was a serious concern for the United States. The vast territory of Louisiana was originally claimed by France, transferred to Spain in 1762, and then returned to France in 1801. It was feared that they may cut off American trade throughout the region by closing the port at New Orleans. In 1802, the Spanish—who then controlled New Orleans in the name of France—declared that Americans would no longer be allowed to store goods at the vital port.

President Thomas Jefferson responded by asking to purchase New Orleans from France so he could guarantee access to the Mississippi River for American ships. Surprisingly, France responded by offering to sell the entire territory of Louisiana to the United States. At the time, Napoleon ruled France, and Napoleon was more concerned with Europe. In fact, he would go on to briefly conquer nearly all of Europe.

Jefferson agreed to purchase all of Louisiana from France for the sum of $15 million. With the stroke of the pen, the size of the United States nearly doubled. However, the Louisiana Purchase was not without controversy at the time. Critics wondered if the largely unsettled wilderness was worth so much money.

To defend his decision, Jefferson addressed Congress and delivered a famous speech. He argued that the purchase was essential for peace in North America:

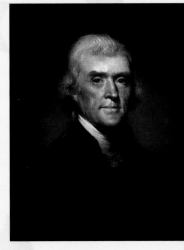

President Thomas Jefferson made the decision to purchase the Louisiana Territory from France in 1803.

> The enlightened government of France saw, with just **discernment**, the importance to both nations of such ... arrangements as might best and permanently promote the peace, friendship, and interests of both ...

> While ... the Mississippi and its waters secure an independent outlet for the produce of the western States, and an uncontrolled navigation through their whole course, free from collision with other powers and the dangers to our peace from that source, the fertility of the country, its climate and extent, promise in due season important aids to our treasury, an ample provision for our posterity, and a wide-spread field for the blessings of freedom and equal laws.

In other words, peace could not be guaranteed if transportation along the Mississippi was threatened. A lasting peace could only exist if the United States controlled the river. Today, the Louisiana Purchase is a key part of Thomas Jefferson's legacy, and few would argue its purchase was anything but wise.

A sea turtle gets a tracking device at a Louisiana animal sanctuary.

The worst hurricane to hit the state was Hurricane Katrina, which struck in August 2005.

In Louisiana, precipitation usually falls in the form of rain. Yearly rainfall in Louisiana averages from 51 inches (130 cm) in the northwest to 66 inches (168 cm) in the southeast. Snow occasionally falls in the north. In winter, frost forms when polar air moves down from Alaska and Canada and settles over the state. From late fall to early spring, farmers must protect their crops from the effects of frost. The growing season is measured by the number of days between the last spring frost and the first fall frost. Farmers statewide enjoy very long growing seasons, up to 290 days in the south.

Wildlife

As naturalist John James Audubon noted, the variety of Louisiana's wildlife seems endless. Many types of trees, shrubs, and grasses thrive in the fields and marshes and along the coast. Wildflowers and other blooms fill the fields in the spring and summer. Deer, black bears, and red wolves live in the pine-filled woods, while catfish, bass, trout, crawfish, and alligators swim in the swamps and rivers. The state's coastal marshes, islands, and beaches are home to brown pelicans, nutrias (a type of rodent), crappies (a type of fish), redear sunfish, and green tree frogs.

An abundance of sea life, including oysters, rays, sharks, speckled trout, and bluefish, lives just offshore in the Gulf. Huge numbers of crabs and shrimp inhabit local waters too. While many plants and animals can be found in abundance, concerned citizens throughout the state are acting to protect Louisiana's rare or endangered species. These include sea turtles, the Louisiana quillwort (a water plant), and birds such as the red-cockaded woodpecker, least tern, and piping plover.

FAST FACT

Louisiana's coast is constantly changing. The coastal land is sinking and sea levels are rising. The situation is so bad that places are disappearing from maps. The National Oceanic and Atmospheric Administration is constantly removing various bays and islands from their maps as they become part of the Gulf of Mexico.

Louisiana's life-giving rivers can also cause serious problems. Every summer, an area that scientists call a "dead zone" forms off the coast of Louisiana. As the Mississippi River flows past farms, it carries away some of the fertilizers that have been used on the farmland. When the river empties into the Gulf of Mexico, the fertilizers are deposited along the coast, contributing to a burst of algae growth. This causes a loss of oxygen in the water. These low oxygen levels kill fish, shrimp, crabs, and other sea life. In recent summers, the size of the dead zone has been close to 8,000 square miles (20,700 sq km)—about the size of New Jersey. To try to fix the problem, people all along the Mississippi River are learning ways to keep fertilizers out of the water. They are building barriers and filters that help prevent fertilizers from spreading into rivers.

Louisiana's Future

Louisiana's long, heavily populated coastline is under threat. Every hour, an area of land the size of a football field sinks under the Gulf of Mexico's waves. In the last hundred years, Louisiana has lost an area of wetlands the size of the state of Delaware! In 2017, Louisiana's governor declared a state of emergency as a result.

Louisiana's coast is shrinking for several reasons. One major one is called subsidence. This is what scientists call the sinking of a large area of land. Subsidence is a natural process. However, many scientists think that humans are speeding it up in Louisiana by extracting natural gas and oil from underneath the ground. Rising sea levels also threaten Louisiana's coast. In the coming years, sea levels are expected to continue rising. This will put even more of Louisiana's coast underwater. It remains to be seen how much Louisiana's lawmakers can slow this shrinking of the state's coast.

Projected Louisiana land loss

Source: Coastal Protection and Restoration Authority
Graphic: Los Angeles Times

This map shows the land that experts believe will disappear due to the extraction of oil and natural gas.

What Lives in Louisiana?

Louisiana iris

Southern live oak

Flora

Louisiana Iris   Louisiana's state wildflower is the Louisiana iris. This name refers to five different species of irises that are native to the state. They bloom in a variety of colors and are planted in gardens across the country due to their beautiful flowers.

Longleaf Pine   This pine tree is threatened across the United States. Longleaf pine forests once covered most of the Southeast, but they are now limited to small, isolated areas. Longleaf pines begin their life in a grasslike form before growing a trunk and growing to heights of 120 feet (37 m). Many animals that call longleaf pine forests home are also threatened because of their limited habitat.

Partridge Pea   The partridge pea is a wildflower that is native to Louisiana. It is an annual—meaning its life cycle is just one growing season. The plant's flowers are large and yellow. It is an important source of food for many birds that live in Louisiana.

Southern Live Oak   The southern live oak is an iconic tree in the Deep South. Its range is a narrow band stretching along the coast of the South. The tree has massive branches that spread out from the trunk. This majestic appearance makes it a popular tree for landscaping, and it can be found planted in historical sites around Louisiana.

Southern Magnolia   The southern magnolia is found across several southern states. It is an evergreen tree (it does not lose its leaves during the winter). The southern magnolia has a distinctive appearance. Its leaves are dark green and leathery, and its large, white flowers are striking.

Fauna

Alligator   Alligators inhabit nearly all of Louisiana. The only other state where this is the case is Florida. The American alligator can grow quite big. Large males can weigh nearly 1,000 pounds (453 kilograms). They are a common sight in bayous and rivers around the state.

Alligator Snapping Turtle   The alligator snapping turtle is a massive freshwater turtle. It can weigh up to 220 pounds (100 kg) and live for up to one hundred years. Although it is ferocious looking, with a large mouth and spiky shell, the alligator snapping turtle generally does not bite people unless provoked.

Alligator snapping turtle

Brown Pelican   The brown pelican is the state bird of Louisiana and is featured on its seal and flag. These birds can also be found along the coast of many other states and even in Central and South America. Brown pelicans feed primarily on fish, which they dive into the water to catch.

Green Tree Frog   The green tree frog is the state amphibian of Louisiana. Its color can vary from a brilliant lime green to a dark, muted green. Green tree frogs are quite small and live on a diet of insects that they catch with their long tongues.

Louisiana Black Bear   The Louisiana black bear is the state mammal of Louisiana and a subspecies of the American black bear. Its longer and narrower skull differentiates it from other American black bears. It used to be listed as an endangered species. However, in 2016 it was removed from the list because its numbers and habitat had recovered significantly.

Louisiana black bear

Earthworks at Poverty Point State Historic Site were built by early residents of Lousiana.

2 The History of Louisiana

Louisiana has a rich, colorful history. Its French roots distinguish it from other states and have shaped its history for centuries, giving rise to traditions like Mardi Gras. The large African American community that calls the state home also made a serious impact on the history of the state—and the world. Jazz music, just one innovation created by members of the African American community, spread from New Orleans to every corner of the world.

Native Americans

Prehistoric groups of people first arrived in present-day Louisiana during the last ice age, about 10,000 BCE. It was a much cooler and drier place then. These people were nomadic hunters, meaning they followed animals they hunted from place to place. As early as 3500 BCE, some built extraordinary mounds of earth. In northern Louisiana, in an area called Watson Brake, scientists have discovered eleven huge mounds that rise up to 25 feet (8 m). Scientists are still puzzled by their purpose.

Natve Americans used dugout canoes like this one to get around.

Millet was an important grain for Native American communities.

In addition to hunting, the prehistoric people fished in the rivers and gathered fruits and nuts. Scientists refer to these tribes as the Mound Builders. In later years, the descendants of Mound Builders used tools, worked metal, and decorated pottery. Some began to stay in one place year-round. They traded with tribes as far away as present-day Wisconsin.

The people who met the European explorers in the sixteenth century were descendants of the Mound Builders. These Native Americans lived along the coast and waterways of southeastern Louisiana. Most were farmers who tended crops of maize, melons, squash, beans, and millet—a type of grain. Men hunted bear, rabbit, deer, and wild turkeys with bows and arrows. But the major sources of food for southern groups were fish, clams, and oysters.

Their villages were groups of homes made from poles and thatched leaves. For transportation, the Native Americans built **dugout canoes** from trees. People wore dyed and painted clothing made from animal skins. Both men and women wore jewelry—anklets, earrings, necklaces, and nose rings. Men and women also wore tattoos that symbolized their achievements in life.

Many different tribes lived across Louisiana. The Tunica and Natchez culture groups were found in the northeast. People who spoke the Muskogean language lived in the central regions. These included the Houma and Choctaw tribes. The Caddo, including the Natchitoches, lived in the northwest. The Chitimacha and Atakapa peoples lived along the coast and swamps of the south.

The Europeans Arrive

In 1519, a Spanish explorer named Alonso Álvarez de Pineda traveled through the region. He reported seeing a river flowing with gold. What he probably saw was the Mississippi River. Another Spanish explorer, Hernando de Soto, undoubtedly explored the Mississippi in 1541. De Soto led an expedition for gold through much of America's southeast. However, he died before his army entered Louisiana. The Europeans brought diseases that quickly spread among the Native population. Many died before the next major contact with European explorers.

In 1682, French explorer René-Robert Cavelier, sieur de La Salle, traveled down the Mississippi River. He claimed the area that now includes Louisiana and some of the neighboring states for the French king, Louis XIV. La Salle named the territory Louisiane in honor of the king.

After La Salle's claim, Pierre and Jean-Baptiste Le Moyne set sail from France and founded an outpost near present-day Biloxi, Mississippi, in 1699. (Notably, Jean-Baptiste would go on to found New Orleans in 1718.) The settlers encountered Native Americans and built forts to protect themselves from the Spanish, who had settled in present-day Florida and Mexico, and the British, who had established colonies along the continent's east coast.

Meanwhile, in Europe, France, Spain, and their allies were at war with Great Britain and its allies. France needed money to support the war effort. Louisiana was not a moneymaking colony for France, so the French government decided to turn it over to private funders. The first permanent settlement was founded in 1714 at present-day Natchitoches.

In 1684, La Salle set sail from France, hoping to return to the mouth of the Mississippi River and start a settlement. The expedition overshot the river, reaching the Texas coast instead.

Beginning in 1717, a Scottish economist named John Law convinced thousands of people to come to Louisiana. Investors in France funded the settlements. Some settlers were prisoners shipped out of France by government officials who did not want these criminals in France. Others were Europeans who were promised land and livestock in exchange for settlement. So many Germans accepted Law's offer that the Mississippi shoreline west of New Orleans became known as the German Coast. Law promised riches. However, the pioneers found the land to be an insect-filled swamp full of deadly tropical diseases and a Native population unhappy about the newcomers' arrival.

Thousands of slaves from West Africa and the French-owned Caribbean islands arrived during that period too. They were forced to work against their will. In addition, the slaves suffered from the intense heat, insects, and disease.

Slaves brought valuable farming knowledge to the land. Tobacco and indigo became cash crops. Yet farming settlements did not make anyone wealthy. The investors stopped paying. Law's company went bankrupt in 1720.

Meanwhile, the Spanish built Fort Los Adaes in northwestern Louisiana. It became the capital of Texas Province in 1729. As European settlements grew and prospered, the colonists took over more and more of the land belonging to the Native people. Many tribes had to fend for themselves or pick a European nation to befriend. Both the Natchez and the Chickasaw groups fought the French. However, the Choctaw stood by the French in many conflicts.

In the mid-1750s, most European powers, including France, were again at war. In North America, the war between France and Great Britain was called the French and Indian War. Many battles were fought on North American soil. By 1762, the French sensed defeat. They did not want to lose their territory to the British. Instead, France gave all its land west of the Mississippi River, plus New Orleans, to its ally Spain. When the war ended in 1763, France surrendered the remainder of its North American territory to Great Britain.

By that time, the first of thousands of French colonists had begun to arrive from Canada. The Acadians had lived on the island of Nova Scotia in eastern Canada for more than a century. In 1755, the British demanded that the Acadians sign a loyalty oath to Great Britain. When the Acadians refused, the British forced them out. Many Acadians traveled thousands of miles to reach the former French colony of Louisiana. There, the Acadian refugees later became known as Cajuns.

Independence from Great Britain

In 1775, the thirteen British colonies along the east coast of America began their fight for independence. The Spanish governor of Louisiana helped the colonists. He allowed goods to travel up the Mississippi River to supply the American revolutionaries. In 1783, the colonies won their independence and became the United States of America. Through a deal with Spain, New Orleans became an important port city for the newly independent nation.

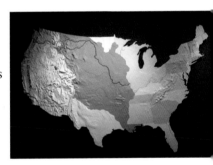

The Louisiana Territory is shown in dark brown.

In 1800, Spain signed a treaty that returned the huge Louisiana Territory to France. The area included all or part of fifteen future states, not just Louisiana. US president Thomas Jefferson worried that France would close New Orleans to American shipping, so the United States bought the territory. This sale, known as the Louisiana Purchase, greatly increased the size of the United States. To make governing the region easier, the

The First Peoples

When French settlers first started exploring Louisiana, they discovered that a variety of people already lived there. The state had more than ten thousand indigenous people living in different tribes. Settlement of the Louisiana region dates back as far as ten thousand years ago. Farming of the land began two thousand years ago. Along the Gulf Coast, the Atakapa lived in the western side of the state, while the Chitimacha lived on the eastern Gulf coast. The Caddo people were located in the western and northern sections of what is now Louisiana. The eastern portion of the land was populated by the Tunica, Natchez, Houma, and Choctaw people. The Choctaw were one of the largest and most dispersed tribes in Louisiana.

While these tribes had different languages and customs, there were also striking similarities between the groups. Most tribes hunted, fished, and farmed. Homes were constructed from tree branches, grasses, and wattle and daub. Almost all tribes had faiths based on the spirituality of nature, and many indigenous people honored their dead with burial mounds.

The Europeans that came to the area borrowed many of the tools Louisiana Natives used, including dugout canoes, baskets made of river cane, blowguns, and more. When the Europeans sought to drive out or assimilate the Native Americans in Louisiana, many used the area's swamps to hide. The United States used some treaties to take land from the local tribes but also forced many to cede their lands and then relocate to what is now Oklahoma. This was called the Trail of Tears, during which an estimated fifteen thousand Native Americans died. Over time, some Native Americans made their way back to the state and rebuilt their lives. Some tribes continue to speak their original languages to this day.

Today, there are four federally recognized tribes in Louisiana, including the Chitimacha Tribe of Louisiana, the Coushatta Tribe of Louisiana, the Jena Band of Choctaw, and the Tunica-Biloxi Tribe of Louisiana. In addition, the

A map of the Trail of Tears

state itself recognizes ten tribes. They are the Addai Caddo Tribe, the Biloxi-Chitimacha Confederation of Muskogee, the Choctaw-Apache Community of Ebarb, the Clifton Choctaw, the Four Winds Tribe Louisiana Cherokee Confederacy, the Grand Caillou/Dulac Band, the Isle de Jean Charles Band, the Louisiana Choctaw Tribe, the Point-Au-Chien Tribe, and the United Houma Nation.

Spotlight on the Choctaw

The Choctaw are descendants of the Muskogean people, a mound-building society that lived in the Mississippi River valley for more than one thousand years before the Europeans arrived.

George Catlin painted this portrait of a Choctaw woman in 1834.

Clans   Within the Choctaw tribe, there were two groups: the elders and the youth. Both groups had several clans, called *iskas*. A child was born into the *iska* to which his or her mother belonged. Fathers had limited control over their children. In Choctaw society, a child's oldest maternal uncle looked after him or her.

Homes   Choctaw winter houses were circular, made with wood frames, and covered with mud. The roofs were made from tree bark and grasses. Summer houses were rectangular, with two holes on either end that let air flow in and out easily.

Choctaw women gather to make baskets together.

Food: The Choctaw were excellent farmers. Corn was their main crop, but they also grew other vegetables. Men hunted deer, turkeys, rabbits, and other small animals.

Clothing   Early female Choctaw clothing consisted of blouses and short skirts made of animal hide. Men wore breechcloths (loincloths). Both men and women often went barefoot at home. In later days, women wore blouses and skirts made of cotton material.

Art   The Choctaw were known for making beautiful baskets. They were made with river cane and palmetto grass, and then dyed with plant dye. These baskets were used in food preparation, storage, and given as gifts.

Magic Sand

Many people think of swamps when they think of Louisiana. Yet the state is also home to a number of beautiful sand beaches. Both along the Gulf of Mexico and inland lakes, there are long stretches of sandy beach where people come to vacation and relax.

You can use sand from the beach to create your own cool toy: magic sand. Magic sand looks just like normal sand until you place it in water. Then it acts quite strangely! To make your own magic sand, follow the simple steps below.

Materials

- A cup of sand (natural or colored sand will work)
- Scotchgard fabric and upholstery protector spray
- Tin foil

Directions

1. To begin, tear off a section of tin foil that is at least 2 feet (61 cm) long.
2. Spread out the sand in an even layer on the foil. Try to make sure there are no large clumps or thick parts in the sand.
3. Spray the Scotchgard back and forth across the sand. The sand should appear wet from the spray. If it does not, reapply more Scotchgard.
4. Let the sand dry.
5. Once it is dry, break it apart and mix it together.
6. Spread it back out and spray it once more.
7. Repeat this process four or five times to ensure that all of your sand is coated in Scotchgard.
8. Once you break the sand apart for the last time, you have magic sand!
9. The Scotchgard is hydrophobic—that means it repels water. As a result, your magic sand acts very strangely when exposed to water. Rather than mixing with it, it remains separate. Try playing around with your sand in the water and see what happens!

territory was divided. One part was called the Territory of Orleans. This area included most of present-day Louisiana.

Early Statehood

By 1810, the future state's population grew to more than seventy-six thousand people. New steam-powered ships began traveling the Mississippi River, carrying tons of goods and supplies to and from the expanding nation. New Orleans became the seventh-largest city in the United States. On April 30, 1812, Louisiana became the eighteenth state.

In the early 1800s, pirates were operating in the Caribbean Sea. Many brought stolen goods to New Orleans to sell. Some pirates, known as privateers, were given permission by the United States to attack any non-American ship. The British began fighting the privateers. They also started kidnapping American sailors and invading American waters. In response, the United States declared war on Great Britain in 1812.

Pirate Jean Lafitte

During the War of 1812, British generals saw the importance of New Orleans as a seaport and planned an attack. They invited one of the most notorious pirates, Jean Lafitte, to join their navy. But Louisiana's governor ordered a raid on Lafitte's harbor at Barataria Bay and captured his brother Pierre. Meanwhile, General Andrew Jackson prepared to defend the city from the British with whoever was willing to fight, including Choctaw warriors and free African Americans. Jean Lafitte gathered other pirates to help Jackson's troops in return for Pierre's freedom. On January 8, 1815, General Jackson's motley army defeated a British force that was twice its size. What came to be known as the Battle of New Orleans was a great victory. (Little did the opposing armies know that two weeks

The Battle of New Orleans took place in 1815.

earlier, the United States and Great Britain had signed a treaty that ended the war.) Andrew Jackson became a national hero and was elected president of the United States in 1828.

A Booming Economy

Large Louisiana farms, or plantations, became very profitable in the first half of the nineteenth century. Cotton grew well in the northern part of the state, and sugar thrived in the south. White landowners operated the plantations and used black slaves to perform the hard labor of planting and harvesting crops. Some white landowners grew wealthy as a result of slave labor and the ease with which they could ship their crops up and down the Mississippi River. One of these people was Zachary Taylor. He made Baton Rouge his adopted home before being elected US president in 1848. A year later, the city became the capital of Louisiana.

New Orleans thrived as the second-busiest port in the United States. From 1820 to 1860, hundreds of thousands of immigrants arrived from Europe, South America, and the Caribbean. The city had more free blacks than any other city in the United States. Life became a mix of many cultures. In 1834, the Medical College of Louisiana (later renamed the University of Louisiana, then Tulane University) was founded in the city.

The Civil War

Slavery was a major topic of debate in the United States in the first half of the nineteenth century. Most people living in Northern states wanted to abolish, or end, slavery. But Southern states relied on slavery to support their economy.

In 1860, Abraham Lincoln, an antislavery politician, was elected president. South Carolina

This print shows the capture of New Orleans during the Civil War.

decided to secede, or withdraw, from the United States (the Union). Louisiana was one of ten other Southern states that, in 1861, also seceded. These states formed the Confederate States of America. Lincoln refused to accept the withdrawal of these Southern states from the Union.

In April 1861, Confederate soldiers fired on and captured Fort Sumter in South Carolina. It was the start of the Civil War, which would continue for four years. Few battles took place within Louisiana. Early in the war, Union troops occupied New Orleans and Baton Rouge, taking control of the ports and most of the lower Mississippi River boat traffic. The Union army declared New Orleans the capital of all the Union-controlled land in Louisiana. Louisiana's Confederate government moved its capital from Baton Rouge to Shreveport. Thousands of escaped slaves joined the Union army. Many were organized into **regiments** to defend New Orleans and other key cities. The Confederacy eventually lost the war. In April 1865, General Robert E. Lee of the Confederacy surrendered to General Ulysses S. Grant of the Union. Later that year, Louisiana was one of thirty states that approved the Thirteenth Amendment to the US Constitution, which abolished slavery in the United States.

Reconstruction and Jim Crow

Louisiana was a different place after the Civil War. Crops and farms were ruined, homes

A riot in Louisiana during Reconstruction

were destroyed, schools were empty, roads were unusable, and banks and other businesses failed. Angry at the loss of their old way of life, many Southerners resented Northerners who came to the South. They called them "carpetbaggers" because their traveling bags were made from carpets.

Though slaves were now free, Louisiana and other Southern states passed new laws known as Black Codes. These codes took away many of the rights promised to African Americans, such as the freedom to have certain jobs or live in certain places. In July 1866, a group of politicians met in New Orleans to discuss issues including voting rights. A crowd of white people, including police officers, killed more than thirty black people and several of their white supporters.

This incident and other events led the US Congress to pass the first of several laws called the Reconstruction Acts. The acts put the former Confederate states under US Army control. Like the other states, Louisiana could not return to the Union as a state without drafting and accepting a new state constitution. Louisiana citizens adopted a new constitution that gave some rights to members of all races and voting rights to black men. The constitution also called for at least one public school in every parish. All children ages six to eighteen could attend, no matter the color of their skin. On June 25, 1868, Louisiana was officially readmitted as a state.

Louisiana during this time took bold steps forward and suffered violent reactions. John W. Menard was the first African American elected to Congress. But the 1868 election results were disputed, and he was never seated. In 1872, P. B. S. Pinchback briefly served as governor, the first African American to hold that office. Some white Louisianans fought such changes with **intimidation** and violence. They joined

Horatio Bateman's artistic representation of Reconstruction shows historical figures working together to rebuild America.

organizations such as the White League and the Ku Klux Klan. These groups terrorized African Americans and the whites who supported equal opportunities for African Americans.

In 1877, federal control of Reconstruction ended in Louisiana. The army left and new politicians came into power. They did very little to help Louisianans because they believed that was not the government's role. Much of the progress made during Reconstruction was stopped.

Life in the countryside remained difficult. Many people found jobs mining sulfur or salt or harvesting pine and cypress for lumber. More than sixty towns grew around lumber companies in Louisiana. Other towns grew along the newly built railroads that ran through the delta. Farmers from the Northeast and Midwest produced an abundance of rice in the prairies of southwest Louisiana.

P. B. S. Pinchback served as Louisiana's governor from December 1872 to January 1873, becoming the first African American governor in the nation.

However, many more landowners could not afford to run their plantations now that slaves no longer provided free labor. Their solution was a system called sharecropping. Black and white farm laborers worked a portion of the land and gave a percentage of their earnings to the landowner. Usually money did not exchange hands. Instead, landowners would provide the sharecroppers with tools, food, and supplies on credit during the planting and growing seasons. When it was time to split the earnings after crops were harvested, most of the sharecroppers' portion went to the landowner to pay off the loans. Many former slaves found themselves working the same land and living in the same houses as they had before they were free.

By the end of the nineteenth century, nearly all the rights granted to African American citizens in Louisiana had been taken away. White politicians who controlled the government passed many "Jim Crow" laws. These laws called for separation of the races in schools, in public places, and in public transportation. In 1891, a group of black leaders in New Orleans decided to challenge the laws. The next year, Homer Plessy, a shoemaker of black descent, boarded a whites-only train car and was arrested. The case went all the way to the US Supreme Court. The court ruled that segregation laws were legal as long as they provided for "equal" service to blacks and whites. The 1896 decision was a major setback to African Americans in their struggle for equal rights.

In 1898, a new state constitution required that black men must own property, be able to read and write, and pay a fee (called a poll tax) before they could vote. However, white men did not need to meet these requirements to vote. (At the time, no women were allowed to vote.) It would be many years before black Louisianans were given equal rights.

The Twentieth Century

The new century brought a new industry— **petroleum**. After oil was found near Jennings in 1901, oil wells sprang up across the southern part of the state and later in the northwest near Shreveport and Bossier City. Pipelines were built to send oil from fields in Texas and Oklahoma to the port at Baton Rouge.

In 1927, heavy rains caused weeks of flooding along the banks of the Mississippi River between Missouri and the Gulf of Mexico. In Louisiana, the water broke through the levees that landowners had built in the lowlands. The river rose nearly 50 feet (15 m) at Baton Rouge. Hundreds of thousands of people were left homeless. Millions of dollars' worth of property was destroyed.

In 1928, Huey P. Long was elected governor of Louisiana. A year later, the United States entered a period of severe economic hardship known as the Great Depression. Millions of Americans were out of work. Long created jobs for Louisiana farmers who could not find employment elsewhere. They worked on large public improvement projects, such as roads, schools, and flood-control programs. Long taxed wealthy citizens and large corporations. He used the money to run social programs, such as providing free textbooks to public school students.

When the United States entered World War II in 1941, Louisiana farmers and factory workers provided much-needed supplies. The state was rich with oil and minerals that were important to the war effort. For the first time in the state's history, there were more citizens working in the cities than in rural areas. Baton Rouge nearly quadrupled in size. While men were fighting overseas, women worked in factories and in other jobs that used to be off-limits to them. The shipyards in New Orleans built many vessels for use in the war. After the war, the boom times in the cities continued. New tax laws invited more and more industry to the state.

Circumstances also started to improve for African Americans. The US Supreme Court ruled in 1954 on a case that started in Kansas, called *Brown v. Board of Education of Topeka*. The Court overturned the earlier decision in Homer Plessy's case and said that it was not possible to have separate but equal schools for black children and white children. All schools had to be open to children of all races. The 1954 decision applied only to schools. Yet it was an important legal step toward ending many other types of segregation—for example, on buses and trains, and in restaurants and other public places. Change did not come right away. But the 1954 decision gave hope to black citizens, who would see many of their civil rights restored over the next decades.

New Iberia, Louisiana, during the 1927 floods

Huey P. Long served as Louisiana's governor from 1928 to 1932 and then served as a senator from 1932 to 1935.

Post-War Years

Louisiana enjoyed decades of **prosperity** after World War II. Oil provided a lot of money and jobs for the state. But in the 1980s, oil prices declined around the world. Louisiana went into another depression. To try to regain lost income, the state looked to its unique heritage. The government promoted tourism in the state. It also changed its gambling laws to allow riverboat casinos to open near New Orleans, Baton Rouge, Lake Charles, and Shreveport. From 1994 to 1999, tourism grew more in Louisiana than in any other state.

Billions of dollars in increased income earned from tourism and gambling helped the state in many ways. One area was the improvement of the public school system. In the late 1990s, Louisiana began repairing or replacing aged school buildings and raised teachers' salaries.

Hurricane Katrina and Its Aftermath

Tragedy struck on August 29, 2005, when Hurricane Katrina raged over southeast Louisiana. Rain and strong winds created huge ocean waves that pounded New Orleans. Water levels rose in Lake Pontchartrain, just north of New Orleans, pouring water over the city's levees. Eventually some levees broke. Four-fifths of New Orleans was flooded. The southeast section, called the Lower Ninth Ward, and nearby St. Bernard Parish were almost entirely underwater.

About 1,500 people died. Around 900,000 lost their homes. Thousands flocked to shelters set up in the Superdome, the city's convention center, and other places. They waited for days for any kind of assistance. Clean drinking water and food were hard to find. The government was slow to provide relief. After help arrived, some people settled in nearby cities. A quarter of New Orleanians left for Texas and other neighboring states. Many people never came back.

New Orleans after Hurricane Katrina in 2005

Cleanup required a lot of hard work. The leftover debris could have filled the Superdome thirteen times. People from across the nation and the world came to help Louisiana, and residents began rebuilding levees, schools, other public buildings, and homes. In a matter of years, New Orleans became one of America's fastest-growing cities. Still, that was growth from a very low starting point. It might be many years yet before the population of New Orleans returns to its pre-Katrina level.

A Troubled Past and Bright Future

Like most states in the South, Louisiana has a complicated relationship with its past. Statues around the state used to celebrate the leaders of the Confederacy. Even though these leaders attempted to leave the United States, they were celebrated. The ideas they fought for—of racial superiority and slavery—were often ignored.

In 2015, New Orleans helped lead the charge across the nation to change this. The city

The Superdome sheltered thousands during Hurricane Katrina.

Louisiana's Important People

Louis Armstrong

Born in 1901 in New Orleans, Armstrong had a difficult early life in the city. He moved between family members before ending up in a group home due to run-ins with the law. There, he received trumpet lessons that complemented what he had already taught himself about music. He went on to become one of the most famous jazz musicians in history. He was known around the world for his gravelly voice and impressive trumpet solos.

Louis Armstrong

Kate Chopin

Although she was born in Missouri, Kate Chopin moved to Louisiana after she graduated from college. She wrote many short stories and novels that soon made her famous. Most of her writing was set in her adopted home of Louisiana. She also wrote about themes that were relevant to life in the South, such as race.

Kate Chopin

Al Copeland

Al Copeland was a famous restauranteur who was born in New Orleans. He founded the Popeyes Chicken & Biscuit chain that quickly spread across the country. As of 2016, there were more than 2,600 locations around the world, and its name had changed to "Popeyes Louisiana Kitchen." Copeland also owned more upscale restaurants in the New Orleans area and was a well-known resident of the city.

Michael DeBakey

This famous surgeon was born in Lake Charles in 1908 and went to school at Tulane University to become a doctor. Throughout his career in medicine, he made many important breakthroughs. He invented medical devices that have helped many people live longer, healthier lives. One of his most famous inventions is a pump that helps people with failing hearts stay alive.

Michael DeBakey

Mahalia Jackson

Mahalia Jackson was born in New Orleans in 1911. Her beautiful voice led her to become a famous gospel singer. She was inducted into the Grammy Hall of Fame for her extensive recordings. Jackson also used her fame to lend support to the civil rights movement of the 1960s. As an African American woman of national recognition, she was an important ally to leaders like Martin Luther King Jr.

Madam C. J. Walker

Huey P. Long

Huey Long was born in 1893 in a small town in Louisiana. He was elected governor of Louisiana at the age of thirty-four. Long appealed to the rural poor of Louisiana—in doing so he alienated many middle- and upper-class Louisianans. He was later accused of corruption by various political enemies before his assassination at the age of forty-two.

Jelly Roll Morton

Born Ferdinand Joseph LaMothe, this African American pianist is much better known by his stage name, Jelly Roll Morton. He was a major figure in the early history of jazz. Morton even claimed to have invented jazz, although many other musicians did not agree with this.

Madam C. J. Walker

Born as Sarah Breedlove in 1867, she was first of her siblings born into freedom after the end of slavery. From these humble beginnings, she built a business empire selling beauty products for African American women: Madam C. J. Walker Manufacturing Company. Throughout her life, she used her riches to promote social causes and contribute to charities.

Mayor Mitch Landrieu spoke out about the need to remove Confederate monuments from New Orleans.

council voted to remove a number of prominent Confederate monuments. However, they were not actually taken down until two years later. In May of 2017, workers removed three monuments from the streets of New Orleans despite protests from some residents.

New Orleans mayor Mitch Landrieu gave a speech about the need for Louisiana—and the country—to confront its troubled past. He spoke out against the racism that the Confederate monuments stood for, saying, "New Orleans is truly a city of many nations, a melting pot, a bubbling cauldron of many cultures … But there are also other truths about our city that we must confront. New Orleans was America's largest slave market: a port where hundreds of thousands of souls were brought, sold and shipped up the Mississippi River to lives of forced labor [and] misery."

Mayor Landrieu's speech made national news. At a time when some politicians across the South supported symbols of hate and racism, he took a stand. The people of Louisiana were not shying away from their history. They were confronting it head on and standing up for justice. Louisiana is a model for what is possible when people want to move forward together.

Louisiana is known around the world for its Mardi Gras celebrations. Unlike in most states, Mardi Gras is an official holiday in Louisiana. Many state employees are given the day off work.

Mardi Gras takes place the day before the Catholic holiday of Ash Wednesday. Ash Wednesday marks the beginning of a period of fasting—or eating less food than usual. By contrast, Mardi Gras and the days leading up to it are marked by feasting and celebration.

Mardi Gras

The most famous Mardi Gras celebrations take place in New Orleans, although other cities in Louisiana also mark the occasion. In New Orleans, days of parades and parties lead up to Mardi Gras itself. Fantastically decorated floats go through the streets of the city while crowds of people watch. Tourists from around the world flock to the city to experience the chaotic celebration.

Mardi Gras parades feature elaborate floats.

Many different traditions are associated with Mardi Gras. Partygoers typically dress in bright costumes of purple, green, and gold. They also usually wear masks. People on the parade floats throw necklaces of beads, cups, and stuffed animals into the crowds of people lining the street.

Mardi Gras marks the end of the Carnival season, which begins on the sixth of January. From this date, you can purchase a king cake in bakeries around the state. King cakes are a Mardi Gras tradition in Louisiana. A small figurine of the baby Jesus is baked into each king cake. One lucky person then finds the figurine in their cake as they eat it.

King cakes have a surprise inside!

A principal visits a Louisiana classroom. Young people make up about one-fourth of Louisiana's population.

3 Who Lives in Louisiana?

The state of Louisiana is home to people of all backgrounds and races. Due to its history, it is a diverse melting pot of cultures. Bustling communities of people who trace their heritage to places all around the world call the state home. No matter the color of their skin or the language they speak, all of these people are Louisianan through and through. Pride in the state runs high.

A History of Immigration

In the beginning, the relationship between Native Americans and European colonists was often peaceful. The Native Americans taught the European settlers many secrets to survival. These included which vegetables to grow, how to cook with native herbs and spices, where to fish and trap, and how to navigate the winding waterways by canoe. By the early eighteenth century, life was different. European diseases and violence between the tribes and colonists destroyed much of the Native population. The Native Americans who survived moved to remote communities in the region or west to new territories. Today in Louisiana, there are only four small reservations

> **FAST FACT**
> During the time of slavery, Louisiana was notable in American history for its large population of free black people. Even then, there was a thriving community of wealthy blacks in cities like New Orleans. As of 2016, 32 percent of Louisianans are black. This is the second-highest percentage of any state.

Creole women enjoy
time together in 1935.

for Native Americans that are recognized by the federal government.

However, Native American influence can be seen in hundreds of place names, such as Atchafalaya, Natchitoches, and Kisatchie. The word "bayou" comes from the Choctaw word *bayuk*, which means "small stream." Another sign of indigenous traditions in Louisiana culture is lagniappe (pronounced LAN-yap). In Louisiana, lagniappe is a little something extra that a shopkeeper or waiter sometimes gives a customer without charging for it. The Spanish picked up the word *yapa* from the Incas of South America, who used the word *yapa* to describe a little bonus given when trading. Many Louisianans believe lagniappe encourages goodwill and friendship.

The Spanish followed the French into Louisiana. Together, the two European groups built a culture that came to be known as Creole, from a Spanish word for people of mixed backgrounds. Wealthy French and Spanish nobles moved to Louisiana and brought European-style art, music, and theater. They built gardens, parks, plantation **manors**, elegant townhomes, symphony and opera halls, and museums. To be Creole in the early days of the colony meant to be born in Louisiana of only Spanish and French heritage. But as Europeans, Native Americans, and African Americans intermarried, being Creole came to mean a person born in Louisiana who had a mixture of French, Spanish, and other

backgrounds. Some
people still speak
a Creole version
of French.

Many blacks
arrived in Louisiana
from West Africa
as slaves in the late
1600s and early 1700s.
Others came from
Caribbean islands as
free persons of color.
Free people of color

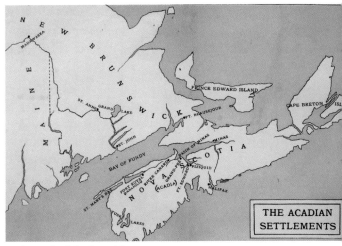

Many Acadians migrated
from Canada and
Maine to Louisiana.

were often skilled artisans, such as the blacksmiths
who created the ironwork that adorns buildings
throughout the state. Some were highly educated.
The Africans who arrived as slaves also brought
customs and beliefs from their native cultures.
At the time, the area was still under French law,
which declared Sundays and religious holidays to
be days of rest—even for slaves. On Sundays and
holidays, Africans gathered in public and private
meeting places. They sold food they had grown and
crafts they had made. They practiced West African
religious rituals and enjoyed the music, storytelling,
and dance of their homelands. Congo Square in
present-day Louis Armstrong Park in New Orleans
is one such former public gathering place. Many
music scholars believe Congo Square was where
the musical style known as jazz was first heard.

In the early part of the eighteenth century,
German farmers settled along the Mississippi
River. French Acadians arrived later in the
century, followed by people from the French
Caribbean colony of Saint-Domingue (now the
country of Haiti). Spanish-speaking people came
from the Canary Islands (located off the northwest
coast of Africa). Called Isleños, they settled in
St. Bernard and Plaquemines Parishes. Irish,

Shops in "Little Vietnam," New Orleans

English, and Scottish immigrants began arriving from the Appalachian region. At the end of the nineteenth century, Italians, most from Sicily, immigrated to Louisiana.

In the twentieth century, immigrants arrived from Latin America and Asia. Louisiana had long had a Hispanic population from the Canary Islands or other Spanish colonies. But many newer arrivals come from Mexico. The largest Asian population has come from Vietnam. In the 1970s, during and after the Vietnam War, Catholic churches throughout the state sponsored Vietnamese refugees. Many came to Louisiana to start new lives. Some who had fished and caught shrimp in Asia found the same jobs there. In the twenty-first century, Vietnamese immigration to Louisiana has slowed, but thousands of new residents have come from India, China, and the Philippines.

North Louisiana

Louisiana is often separated into north and south. The regions differ in geography and in culture. In northern Louisiana, most residents are of British American or African American heritage. However, there are smaller groups, such as Czechs, Germans, Italians, and Hungarians. Farming, ranching, and forestry have been traditional ways of life in the region. Natural gas and oil production have become important as well. Large cotton plantations once lined the valuable farmland along the riverbanks known as the "front lands." In remote swamps and waterways, people struggled to earn a living in the region called the "back lands." There, many still hunt, fish, and trap for income. Today, people who enjoy hunting, boating, and fishing think of the back lands as a special destination.

Set along the Red River, Shreveport is the largest city in northern Louisiana. Shreveport

Louisiana State University

Louisiana's Biggest Colleges and Universities

(Enrollment numbers are from US News and World Report 2018 college rankings.)

1. Louisiana State University, Baton Rouge
(26,118 undergraduate students)

2. University of Louisiana at Lafayette
(15,998 undergraduate students)

3. Southeastern Louisiana University, Hammond
(13,559 undergraduate students)

University of Louisiana at Lafayette

4. Louisiana Tech University, Ruston
(11,281 undergraduate students)

5. Northwestern State University of Louisiana, Natchitoches
(8,700 undergraduate students)

6. University of Louisiana Monroe
(7,778 undergraduate students)

7. McNeese State University, Lake Charles
(6,961 undergraduate students)

Tulane University

8. University of New Orleans
(6,442 undergraduate students)

9. Tulane University, New Orleans
(6,377 undergraduate students)

10. Nicholls State University, Thibodaux
(5,647 undergraduate students)

boomed in the 1830s after steamboat captain Henry Shreve cleared the Red River of a logjam called the Great Raft. The Great Raft stretched more than 150 miles (240 km). Removing the logjam opened up the river to boat traffic. During the Civil War, the city was the capital of Confederate Louisiana. Today, Shreveport is a busy, multicultural center for tourism, commerce, and manufacturing. It has become known as "Hollywood South" for the many movies filmed there.

Farther east is Grambling State University, a historically black college founded in 1901. South of Grambling is a former Native American trading post, Natchitoches. It is the oldest settlement in Louisiana. The city of Alexandria, near the geographic center of the state, also is the divide between cultural regions. The area is known as "the crossroads."

South Louisiana

Southern Louisiana has very deep French and Catholic roots. Yet the region also has influences from Spain, West Africa, the Caribbean, Mexico, Central America, and many parts of Europe and Asia, as well as from Native Americans. One group in particular has fashioned its own unique society. The region of the southwestern prairies and coastal bayous is known as Acadiana, the home of the Cajuns. Though many now work in offices, factories, oil fields, and other businesses, the Cajuns were traditionally fisherfolk and farmers with a strong love of music, food, and family life.

African Americans, Germans, and people from Great Britain also migrated to the area. Many of the newcomers adopted the Cajun way of life. Today, Lake Charles is a thriving modern city located in Acadiana. The city of Lafayette,

Bread Pudding

Louisiana is famous for its Creole-style bread pudding. Restaurants around the state, especially in New Orleans, all have their own take on this classic dish. You can make this bread pudding recipe at home. Once you get the hang of it, you can try adding different ingredients like canned pineapple or sweetened flaked coconut to come up with your own special recipe.

Ingredients:

- 3 ounces of day-old French or Italian bread (about 1/4 of a loaf)
- 1 cup of whole milk
- 1 cup of heavy cream
- 2 eggs
- 1/3 cup of sugar
- 1 teaspoon vanilla extract
- 1 tablespoon of butter

Directions:

1. Whisk the eggs in a mixing bowl.
2. Add the whole milk, heavy cream, sugar, and vanilla extract to the mixing bowl and whisk until the ingredients are combined.
3. Pour the mixture into a small baking dish.
4. Cut the bread into 1-inch cubes and place them in the liquid. Make sure they are submerged.
5. Cover your baking dish and place it in the refrigerator for at least three hours—it is best if it is left overnight.
6. Take the baking dish out of the refrigerator and let it sit at room temperature for an hour or two.
7. Cut the butter into very thin slices and lay it on top of the bread pudding.
8. Preheat the oven to 315°F.
9. Place your small baking dish into a large baking dish with about half an inch of water in it. Put both baking dishes into the oven and cook for an hour. The pudding should set (not be liquid or completely solid but jiggle slightly when you move the dish). Now you can enjoy your very own bread pudding!

A Melting Pot of Cultures and Languages

In the middle of the eighteenth century, French-speaking refugees from Acadia (a region of Canada) flooded into Louisiana during the French and Indian War. These Acadians changed their lifestyle to adapt to the climate of Louisiana, which was so different from their former home in Canada. The Acadians gradually became known as Cajuns—a distinct group of people that still live in Louisiana.

A separate people of French descent also took shape in Louisiana in those early days: the Creoles. The word "Creole" was originally used to refer to white people of French and Spanish descent who were born and raised in southern Louisiana, especially New Orleans. This set them apart from the French and Spanish immigrants who were still arriving in the New World and had not set down deep roots in the area. Over time, the use of the word "Creole" expanded. Some people used it to refer to people of mixed French, Spanish, African, and Native American ancestry. This is how the word is used outside of Louisiana. In the Caribbean and Latin America, it refers only to those of mixed ancestry and not to white descendants of settlers.

This melting pot of different people gave birth to different ways of speaking French. Some speakers, especially the upper classes, spoke in a way that was quite similar to the French spoken in Europe. This language is known as Colonial French. However, a

Two Cajun men herd cattle near New Iberia.

new variety of French also sprang up when the unique dialect of French spoken by the Acadians mixed with local languages. This is sometimes called Cajun French. Furthermore, a truly unique language was also born in Louisiana, called Louisiana Creole. A creole language is formed by the mixing of two of more other languages. Louisiana Creole was formed by French mixing with the many different African languages of slaves and free people of color. The resulting language is very different from French and includes many words of West African origin.

Today, Louisiana French (an umbrella term for the many varieties of French spoken in the state) is under threat. In 1968, there were an estimated million French speakers in the state. By 2011, that number had dropped to between 150,000 and 200,000. However, many Cajun and Creole people are making efforts to preserve their unique language and heritage around the state.

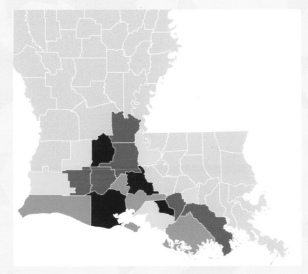

Brown: 20 to 30 percent of the population speaks Cajun French or French

Red: 15 to 20 percent of the population speaks Cajun French or French

Orange: 10 to 15 percent of the population speaks Cajun French or French

Yellow: 4 to 10 percent of the population speaks Cajun French or French

bursting with Cajun restaurants, music clubs, and museums, is one of the cultural centers of the region.

East of Acadiana are the state's largest cities, Baton Rouge and New Orleans. They are also two of the country's largest port cities, with giant docks that are always buzzing with activity, and huge storage facilities.

People in New Orleans take great pride in their city and its rich history. The city is known for its historic buildings with decorative ironwork and lush gardens. Nearly all houses have front porches or stoops. Before air conditioning, many people sat on their porches on hot days to catch any breeze that might blow in from the river.

Cajun Cuisine

In northern Louisiana, food is prepared in much the same way it is in other Southern states. In southern Louisiana, there are two popular ways of cooking: Cajun and Creole.

Gumbo is one very popular dish in Louisiana. It is also a symbol for the diversity of Louisianans. In the earliest days of the colony, the French prized a European recipe for a tasty seafood soup. In Louisiana, they learned to make do with local ingredients, such as shrimp and crawfish. Native Americans added native plants, herbs, and spices to the recipe. The Spanish added hot pepper sauce. African slaves who cooked for the Creole colonists added the vegetable okra. Cajuns contributed tomatoes, turtles, and alligators. Germans added smoked hams and sausages. During Lent (the period between the holy days of Ash Wednesday and Easter), Catholics followed a church rule limiting meat. So vegetables and herbs went into their gumbo recipes. Today, people throughout Louisiana have their own special recipes for gumbo.

Gumbo is one of Louisiana's most famous dishes.

Louisianan Music and Festivals

From farmers' fields, city streets, and backwater bayous to church halls, riverboats, and clubs, the special musical styles of Louisiana ring out. A variety of American musical forms, such as Western swing, blues, and gospel, are heard throughout Louisiana.

When Cajuns first came to Louisiana, they brought Acadian fiddle music. After German farmers moved to Acadiana, they introduced the accordion to their Cajun neighbors. Since then, the accordion has been the soul of Cajun music. African Americans added washboard strumming and other rhythms to the Cajun sound to create the lively dance music called zydeco. New Orleans, meanwhile, has long been famous for jazz. Early stars were Louis Armstrong and Jelly Roll Morton. Louisiana musicians Fats Domino and Jerry Lee Lewis were early rock 'n' roll stars. Today, New Orleans is one of the world's best cities for listening to jazz, blues, rock, gospel, Cajun, zydeco, hip-hop, and more.

Louisiana is rich in festivals. The French expression "Laissez les bon temps rouler," which means "Let the good times roll," is often heard in Louisiana. There are many music festivals. The love of food is revealed in festivals devoted entirely to gumbo, jambalaya, oysters, pralines, meat pies, shrimp, catfish, crawfish, strawberries, and other foods. The ethnic heritage of the state is honored in festivals such as Czech Fest, German Oktoberfest, Laotian New Year, and Isleños Festival.

Fats Domino was one of rock 'n' roll's earliest stars. He was born in New Orleans.

Festivals celebrating religious holidays are also very important to the residents of Louisiana. In December, communities throughout the state celebrate the holiday season with a Festival of Lights. Mardi Gras, which in English means

Celebrities from Louisiana

Hunter Hayes

Hunter Hayes

Hunter Hayes is a country star who was born in the tiny town of Breaux Bridge, Louisiana. When he was just four years old, he started to appear on TV. He rose to fame in 2011 at the age of twenty with his hit single "Wanted." Since then, he was been nominated for five Grammy Awards.

Eli and Peyton Manning

Eli and Peyton Manning are brothers who were born in New Orleans. Their father, Archie Manning, was an NFL quarterback, and both of his sons followed in his footsteps. Both Eli and Peyton led their teams to win two Super Bowls.

Wynton Marsalis

Wynton Marsalis

Wynton Marsalis was born into a New Orleans family of jazz musicians in 1961. He grew up to become a famous trumpeter and jazz composer. Marsalis has won nine Grammy Awards, not only for jazz but also for classical music. He was also the first jazz musician to win the Pulitzer Prize for Music.

Tim McGraw

Tim McGraw

The son of a Major League Baseball player, Tim McGraw grew up in a small town in Louisiana and became a country music superstar. Although his first single was a flop, his second album, *Not a Moment Too Soon*, catapulted him to fame. Since then, he has won three Grammy Awards.

Reese Witherspoon

Reese Witherspoon

Reese Witherspoon was born in New Orleans. Witherspoon appeared in her first movie as a teenager, although she did not become a star until her leading role in *Legally Blonde* (2001). She has starred in numerous movies and TV shows since then.

"Fat Tuesday," is a traditional Roman Catholic carnival that takes place just before Lent begins.

Louisiana's unique blend of ethnic and religious traditions has always helped it stand apart from other states. Citizens are proud of their culture.

A New Trend

Louisiana's population is very diverse in some ways. However, in other ways, the state is less diverse than most of the country. For example, there are very few Hispanic and Asian Americans compared to other states. Hispanics made up just 5 percent of the state's population in the 2016 census. Compare that to a national average of 17.8 percent!

In the future, this is expected the change. The percentage of Hispanics is projected to rise as more people move to the state. By contrast, the percentage of white and African American Louisianans is expected to decline.

The population of the state as a whole is expected to increase. Most of this growth will occur in New Orleans, which currently still has fewer people than it did before Hurricane Katrina struck in 2005.

A Native American dancer performs during the New Orleans Jazz & Heritage Festival in 2015.

This oil production platform is part of Louisiana's southernmost port, Port Fourchon.

4 At Work in Louisiana

Louisiana's economy boasts many different industries. Some of the largest include farming, oil, natural gas, and fishing. Tourism and transportation—driven by the state's location at the mouth of the Mississippi River—are also important. Nevertheless, the economy of Louisiana has suffered in recent years due to a variety of reasons. In February of 2016, the state's chief economist said, "For all practical purposes, Louisiana is in its own **recession**." Falling oil prices have battered the energy industry, which is vital to the state. The tourism industry also suffered after Hurricane Katrina, although it has rebounded in recent years. Despite these difficult conditions, new industries and the creativity of Louisianans make for a hopeful economic future.

Agriculture

Louisiana is blessed with rich soil and a climate that is ideal for growing a variety of crops. The major crops are cotton, sugar, rice, corn, and soybeans. There are about 8 million acres (3.2 million ha) of farmland in the state. Louisiana's crops are sold throughout the country.

FAST FACT
Louisiana's four Native American reservations are home to many different business enterprises. From fish-processing plants to casinos, reservations make a significant contribution to the state's economy. Their museums and cultural attractions also draw tourists—and their money—to the state.

Rice and crawfish fields
in Saint Martin's Parish

Rice is an important crop to Louisiana farmers. Enslaved Africans first brought rice seed to the Louisiana prairies as early as 1718. Rice grew well in the wet soil, but it did not become popular until after the Civil War. In the 1800s, Cajun and German rice farmers used floodwaters from the Mississippi River to grow rice. Residents later developed irrigation channels to provide the water for the crop. In the 1950s, rice farmers added crawfish to their flooded fields. After the farmers harvested the rice, the crawfish would eat algae and rotting plant matter. The crawfish could later be harvested for food, providing a second crop. In addition to providing crops, the crawfish rice fields have become important wetlands for wildlife.

More than a quarter of Louisiana is covered by farms. A third of that land is used for pasture and livestock. Grass grows year-round in the warm, wet climate, so cattle have plenty of fresh grazing land. Farmers also raise hogs and goats. But despite the variety of crops and livestock, fewer people have jobs in farming each year. Large corporations and successful landowners now operate about half of the state's farmland. These large farms earn greater profits and can afford expensive farm machinery. The machines are extremely efficient and do much of the work once done by farm laborers.

Seafood

The seafood industry is an important part of Louisiana's economy. One out of every seventy jobs in the state relates to the industry either directly or indirectly. The industry is also of national importance. Louisiana is the second-biggest producer of seafood in the entire country, behind Alaska. Shrimp, oysters, and crabs are the most important products in the state. Other prized seafood includes red snapper and yellowfin

Boats trawl for shrimp in
Louisiana's waterways.

tuna. Freshwater fishers catch crawfish and catfish. But these creatures are also raised in fish farms.

Louisiana has tens of thousands of jobs in the fishing industry. Besides fishing, people work at selling, shipping, processing, and packaging fish. Thousands of others build and maintain boats, gear, and supplies for the fishing industry.

Timber

Almost half of Louisiana is covered by forests. Pine, oak, sweetgum, cypress, and other trees are harvested. More than twenty-five thousand people have jobs cutting, transporting, or processing timber. Wood in Louisiana is used to make paper, boxes, shopping bags, furniture, and construction materials, as well as baseball bats, musical instruments, and boats. Each year, the forest and forest-products industries add about $4 billion to the economy of the state.

Oil, Natural Gas, and Mining

In the 1870s, companies drilled wells in search of water to make ice. One evening, a night watchman at an ice factory in Shreveport felt wind coming from a well that was being drilled. When he lit a match to investigate, he caused an explosion. Natural gas, not water, had been flowing through the pipe. Gas from the well was soon piped to the factory to provide energy for lighting. This was the beginning of Louisiana's oil and natural gas industry.

The first successful oil well in Louisiana was drilled in 1901 near the town of Jennings, a farming community halfway between Lafayette and Lake Charles. Since that time, rice farmers

Crawfish are a Louisiana favorite.

FAST FACT
Louisiana is the only state where crawfish are produced on a massive scale. There are more than a thousand crawfish farmers and over eight hundred crawfish fishermen in the state. Louisiana crawfish are included in many typical dishes in Louisiana, and they are exported across the country.

Bull Bayou Oil
Field in 1920

This New Orleans
oil refinery is part of
Louisiana's bustling
petrochemical industry.

and swamp fishers along the coast have lived and worked side by side with oil workers. After World War II, major oil fields were discovered in the Gulf of Mexico. In 1947, the first drilling platforms were built offshore out of sight of land. Today, Louisiana is the nation's ninth-largest producer of oil.

But the state does not just drill the oil. The state is a very important storage center for oil and natural gas. Massive salt caves have been filled with oil for emergencies. Dozens of pipelines deliver oil and natural gas from Louisiana to states as far away as Wisconsin.

Louisiana's mines provide important minerals such as sulfur and salt. Louisiana has huge underground rock-salt formations. Some are 50,000 feet (15,240 m) deep and stretch for 1 mile (1.6 km) across. In 1862, the nation's first rock-salt mine was dug on Avery Island. Salt is commonly used for cooking, but it also has uses in papermaking, soapmaking, fabric dyeing, and other areas of manufacturing. Around the country, millions of pounds of rock salt are used each winter to deice roads and make them safe for driving.

The Louisiana Gulf Coast is key to the nation's petrochemical industry. Petrochemical refineries are factories that turn crude oil and natural gas liquids into plastics, fertilizers, synthetic (human-made) rubber, and other products.

People in the state also make well-drilling platforms, ships of all sizes, small trucks, telephones, glass, marine radar, clothing, and hundreds of other products.

Transportation

Steamboats began traveling the Mississippi River in 1811, carrying cargo to and from New Orleans. Louisiana has the nation's second-largest number of navigable waterways. Today, there are more than thirty ports in the state. The Port of South Louisiana is the nation's largest by tonnage carried. It spans the area between New Orleans and Baton Rouge. Dry bulk products such as corn from the Midwest can be poured into large holds in a ship and sucked out at their destination. Deepwater docks at these ports have nearby storage facilities for foods such as tropical fruits and coffee beans. Dock areas also have grain silos, oil tanks, and steel yards and lumberyards.

The Gulf Intracoastal Waterway

Using natural rivers and lakes and human-made channels, Louisiana has created an intracoastal waterway. It allows ocean freighters to travel the entire coastline, safe from storms in the Gulf of Mexico. About one in seven jobs in the state depends on its waterways. The ports at Baton Rouge and Lake Charles are also huge contributors to the state's economy.

Tourism

A large portion of tourism in Louisiana is centered in New Orleans. The "Big Easy" is full of world-famous theaters, museums, restaurants, and music clubs. Football fans flock to the Superdome to cheer for the New Orleans Saints. Visitors spent more than $17.5 billion in the city in 2017. Much of the city's tourism spending takes place during the Mardi Gras celebrations.

Many people visit Louisiana to see its amazing architecture. Each year, people come to admire buildings designed in European and Caribbean styles in New Orleans. Throughout the state, visitors can see historic buildings, traditional

FAST FACT

The oil industry is huge in Louisiana. In 2016, more than fifty-six million barrels of crude oil were produced in Louisiana. But the state's location also makes it an important hub for importing oil. It is home to an offshore port that is the only one along the Gulf Coast able to unload oil from the largest tankers.

Nanotechnology in Louisiana

Nanotechnology is a new field of technology that involves manipulating matter on an extremely small scale, typically 1 to 100 nanometers. A nanometer is a unit of measurement that is one billionth the size of a meter and less than one millionth the size of an inch—far smaller than can be seen with the naked eye. It is hoped that nanotechnology may revolutionize a number of different technologies in the future.

Louisiana Tech University (pictured) and Louisiana State University offer classes in nanotechnology, one of the state's growing new fields.

Universities in Louisiana were among the first to offer programs centered on nanotechnology. Louisiana Tech University and Louisiana State University (LSU) both offer courses in the cutting-edge field. Researchers at universities in the state have made many different breakthroughs in utilizing nanotech. For instance, researchers from LSU collaborated with the company Jupiter Fuels to create a new technology related to natural gas. Using nanomaterial, they proved it was possible to convert natural gas to liquid fuel in a more efficient way than the traditional process. One day, this may revolutionize the industry and help the United States become self-reliant when it comes to energy.

Nanotechnology is also very promising in the field of medicine. New materials may allow for much better treatments in the future. In 2014, Dr. Devash Misra at the University of Louisiana at Lafayette created a new kind of **silicone** using nanotechnology. It is much sturdier than typical silicone as well as germ-resistant. In the future, it may allow medical implants to be made that are far superior to the ones used today.

These are just two examples of how nanotech is expected to help diverse fields in the future. The researchers and companies of Louisiana are committed to finding even more applications for this new field of technology.

plantations, and other sites that serve as reminders of the state's past.

A newer addition to the tourism industry is ecotourism. Ecotourism is travel based on viewing nature and wildlife, such as bird-watching or touring a swamp. Most of the continent's migratory birds stop over in the Pelican State. Ecotours of the state's unique regions teach visitors what every resident already knows: Louisiana is a special place.

The New Orleans Saints have played in the Superdome since 1975.

A Budget Crisis

A state's budget is very important to its economy. When a state is deep in debt, it can cause many different problems. The state may struggle to provide services, like transportation, that underpin the economy. Businesses may leave the state to seek better economic conditions elsewhere.

Unfortunately for Louisiana, the state is facing the worst budget crisis in its history. The state is spending millions of dollars more than it has each year. The result is increased debt and uncertainty about the future. In 2017, lawmakers were expecting a $1 billion shortfall for the budget of 2018, meaning they would have to either increase taxes or drastically cut state services. While Republicans and Democrats negotiated on what would happen in the following year, businesses worried that taxes could suddenly rise or services could be cut overnight. Thankfully, Louisianans have a history of pulling together to do what is best for their state. Louisianans are no strangers to hard work, and it's certain that this work ethic will pay off.

The Birthplace of Jazz

Louisiana gave birth to one of America's truly original art forms: jazz. The beginning of jazz is often traced to Congo Square in New Orleans. In the nineteenth century, slaves were allowed to gather there on Sunday. They would play music with roots from West Africa and dance to complicated rhythms.

By the beginning of the twentieth century, this musical tradition had mixed with many other styles of music present in New Orleans. Spanish music from places like Cuba as well as Western classical music were also performed in the city. The blending of these many traditions led to the creation of jazz.

Congo Square

Early jazz was performed with the instruments made popular from the marching songs of the time: the drum, trumpet, clarinet, and saxophone. The piano was also used to provide harmony—the chords, or multiple notes played at once, that underlie a song.

One of jazz's main innovations was the use of improvisation. Improvisation is when musicians are allowed to spontaneously create new music. This often occurs in the middle of a jazz song, when individual musicians have the opportunity to improvise a solo after starting with a previously written melody. Improvisation does not usually occur in classical music, where musicians are expected to play only the notes written on a sheet of music.

From New Orleans, jazz took the United States by storm. It quickly spread across the country. In the early days, it was often white musicians who performed jazz songs, even though the style of music was pioneered by African American musicians. However, black musicians gradually overcame the racism and discrimination of the time to publicly perform jazz.

From the United States, jazz spread internationally. Over the course of the twentieth century, jazz evolved and changed. Genres like smooth jazz and bebop branched out from the early forms of jazz.

Jazz reshaped the way that the world saw music. In the beginning, music critics did not take jazz seriously. As time went by, jazz gained widespread recognition as an original American art form. And it's an art form that draws musicians and fans alike back to where it all began, Louisiana.

The Louisiana State Capitol was completed in 1932.

5 Government

Louisiana's government is similar to that of other states. There is a governor as well as state congresspeople who work together to create laws. These laws are enforced by the courts. State laws can deal with all sorts of issues, including criminal matters, government regulation, and education reform. However, state laws cannot go against laws made in Washington, DC. Likewise, local laws that are passed in cities and parishes around the state cannot go against federal or state law.

Unlike most states that are organized into various counties, Louisiana has parishes. The term "parish" often refers to an administrative district of the Catholic Church. In Louisiana, however, parishes are also districts that the state uses. This is due to the strong Catholic heritage of the state. In the state's early days, the government organized Louisiana along the same lines as the church.

> **FAST FACT**
> As of June 2018, Louisiana is the only state in the Deep South to have a Democratic governor. Democrat John Bel Edwards was sworn in on January 11, 2016. He replaced Republican governor Bobby Jindal, who had finished his second term and was therefore not allowed to run again.

Separation of Powers

The government of Louisiana, like that of the United States, is divided into three branches.

Executive

The governor is the head of the executive branch. The people of Louisiana choose a governor every four years. He or she can serve only two terms in a row. The governor appoints cabinet members and signs bills into law. Other executive-branch offices, including the lieutenant governor, attorney general, and treasurer, are elected positions. A superintendent of education is appointed by the state board of education to oversee the Louisiana Department of Education.

Governor John Bel Edwards took office in 2016.

Legislative

The legislative branch is made up of the state senate, with 39 members, and the state house of representatives, with 105 members. State **legislators** are elected for four-year terms and cannot be elected more than three times in a row. They meet each year for up to sixty working days. When not working at the capitol in Baton Rouge, legislators meet with people in the area they represent. Often, they hold other jobs, too, working as farmers, business owners, pharmacists, and lawyers.

Judicial

The judicial branch is a system of courts made up of the state supreme court, courts of appeal, and district courts. Most trials are decided by district courts. These courts hear criminal cases and settle arguments over laws. The next level is the court of appeals. If someone does not believe he or she received a fair ruling in the district courts, court of appeals judges will hear the reasons and rule on whether to uphold or overturn the district court decision. Some cases are appealed from a court of appeals to the state supreme court for a final ruling. The supreme court has a chief justice

Lawmakers meet at the Louisiana State Capitol to get important work done.

and six associate justices who are each elected from a separate district. Judges in the appeals and supreme courts serve ten-year terms.

Creating a New Law

State senators and representatives, who together are called legislators, create and pass laws. A law can be started in either the state house of representatives or the state senate. To begin, a legislator proposes an idea for a law. Sometimes these ideas come from the state residents whom the legislator represents. The idea is spelled out in a document called a bill. The legislator who proposes it becomes the bill's sponsor. For example, in 2009, Louisiana Representative Nickie Monica wanted to encourage safety in motor vehicles. He proposed a bill that would fine people for not wearing seatbelts. "We know it's going to save lives," he said.

A courtroom in Monroe

A clerk drafted Representative Monica's bill and assigned the bill a number (HB 499). Next, the bill was read aloud in the house. Then, the bill was assigned to a committee to discuss it. During committee meetings, members review bills and listen to people who have come to talk about why they are in favor of or opposed to a certain bill. After the meetings, the committee decides whether to approve the bill. If the committee approves the bill, it is then read out loud again. A bill must be read in each chamber on at least three separate occasions. At this time, all the representatives can debate the bill and suggest changes. Each time a bill is changed, or amended, the representatives vote.

Once Monica's bill passed the house, it moved to the senate. There, it was reviewed by another committee. Once approved by the committee, the bill was amended and voted on. If the senate passes a bill but makes amendments, the bill must

Keeping Up with Politics

In the past, it was necessary to read the newspaper or attend meetings in person to keep up with the news. Then, television and radio brought current events into people's homes. It became easier to get involved in the community. Now, computers, smartphones, and tablets have made it even easier to learn about what is happening around you.

Your local government likely has a presence on all sorts of social media sites. Using these platforms, they can try to persuade voters to see things their way. For example, both the Republican and Democratic Parties of Louisiana have their own Twitter accounts: @LaDemos and @LaGOP. (The Grand Old Party—or GOP— is another name for the Republican Party.) With an adult, you can view these social media accounts and see what is going on in your state. Just remember that they often present articles and viewpoints that are favorable portraits of their own party—and often unfavorable toward their political opponents.

You can ask an adult to show you the Twitter accounts of the Republican and Democratic Parties of Louisiana.

To find the state representatives who represent you and your family, you can go to the website https://www.legis.la.gov/legis/FindMyLegislators.aspx. The site also lists your representatives' contact information. If you have a strong opinion about a current issue, you can get an adult to help you contact them.

be returned to the house for review before being presented to the governor. If the house approves the changes, it delivers the bill to the governor for signature. If the governor signs the bill, it becomes law. Governor Bobby Jindal signed Representative Monica's bill, which became a law known as Act 166 of 2009.

However, the governor may veto, or refuse to sign, a bill. A vetoed bill is sent back to the legislature. There, lawmakers decide whether to let the bill fail or to override the governor's veto and pass the law. To override a veto, both houses must vote in favor of the bill by a two-thirds majority.

The Power of the People

Louisianans have always known the power of the people. Louisiana's citizens and lawmakers realize that everyone's voice is important. Citizens throughout the state's long history have fought for fair and equal rights.

For example, in 1960, a Louisiana first grader and her family spoke out against racial inequality in schools. Ruby Bridges was a young African American girl who had moved to New Orleans with her family. The federal government in Washington, DC, had ordered New Orleans to desegregate its schools. Black students could no longer be kept out of white schools. This angered many white people in the city. On November 14, 1960, six-year-old Ruby Bridges walked beside four federal marshals through an angry crowd of white protesters to enter an all-white elementary school. When she returned to school the next day, she walked into an empty classroom. All the white families had taken their children out of school. Each day after that, Bridges's teacher taught her only student. And each day, Bridges walked past protesters yelling and throwing things at her on

Louisianans make their voices heard at a rally in 2017.

Ruby Bridges is escorted into school in 1960. Bridges was the first black student at a previously all-white school in Louisiana.

the way to school. A year later, the school was fully integrated. Bridges was no longer the only black student in the building. White and black students attended the school together.

Few children are expected to act as bravely as Ruby Bridges, but all students should speak up for what they believe in. Desegregation occurred because people fought for what they believed was right. They voiced their opinions and worked toward equality for all. This work continues today.

Louisianans stand up for what they believe is right in many different ways. In March of 2017, there was a large protest against the proposed construction of an oil pipeline in the state. Protesters peacefully marched to Louisiana's Department of Natural Resources (DNR) building in New Orleans to express their disapproval of the project. Although the project was ultimately approved by the DNR, the protesters had made their opinion known through their actions. Peaceful protests are part of what make Louisiana, and America, a vibrant democracy.

Glossary

corruption	Dishonest actions by an authority figure. One common example of corruption is money traded for favorable treatment by a government official or police officer.
delta	The mouth of a river, where it empties into a larger body of water.
discernment	The ability or act of understanding something well.
dugout canoes	Canoes, or small boats, made by hollowing out a section of tree trunk.
estuary	A partly enclosed body of water where a river mixes with saltwater from the sea it empties into.
humidity	The amount of water vapor present in the air.
intimidation	The act of making someone afraid.
legislators	Lawmakers; legislators include member of the state and national House of Representatives and Senate. These people write and pass legislation, or laws.
manors	Large, magnificent houses that were often built on plantations.
petroleum	The crude oil that occurs under the surface of Earth. It is extracted and processed to make petroleum products like gasoline, jet fuel, motor oil, and asphalt.
prosperity	The condition of being successful when it comes to money.
recession	A major decline in the economy.
regiments	Military units formed of a number of soldiers.
silicone	A wide group of substances that are often rubber-like and resemble plastic.

N
W E
S

NEW ORLEANS AREA

Kenner
Metairie
New Orleans
River Ridge
Jefferson
Chalmette
Westwego
Gretna
Marrero
Harvey

Caddo Lake
Black Bayou
Upper Ouachita National Wildlife Refuge
Handy Brake National Wildlife Refuge
2
2
Minden
Bastrop
D'Arbonne National Wildlife Refuge
Bayou D'Arbonne Lake
Shreveport
20
Monroe
65
DRISKILL MOUNTAIN
Ruston
Bayou Macon
Tallulah
Bayou Lafourche
1
Natchitoches
Red River
167
65
Tensas River National Wildlife Refuge
49
171
71
Black Lake Bayou
Black Lake
84
165
Catahoula National Wildlife Refuge
65
Mississippi River
Kisatchie National Forest
Toledo Bend Reservoir
Sabine River
Catahoula Lake
Bayou Cocodrie National Wildlife Refuge
Alexandria
Fort Polk
Alexander State Forest
Lake Ophelia National Wildlife Refuge
1
TUNICA HILLS
61
55
Bogalusa
165
71
49
Opelousas
New Roads
190
Hammond
12
Bayou Nezpique
Moss Blu
190
Eunice
Baton Rouge
Lake Pontchartrain
Slidell
Sulphur
10
Calcasieu River
Lafayette
1
10
La Place
10
90
Lake Borgne
Lake Charles
Jennings
Crowley
Chandeleur Sound
Breton Wildlife
Sabine National Wildlife Refuge
Lacassine National Wildlife Refuge
Abbeville
New Iberia
Chitimacha Indian Reservation
New Orleans
Calcasieu Lake
Grand Lake
82
INTRACOASTAL WATERWAY
Jean Lafitte National Historic Park
Breton Sound
Cameron Prairie National Wildlife Refuge
Sabine Lake
White Lake
Weeks Bay
Vermilion Bay
90
Morgan City
Raceland
82
Rockefeller State Wildlife Refuge
Marsh Island
Marsh Island State Wildlife Refuge
East Cote Blanche Bay
Atchafalaya Bay
Houma
1
23
Batataria Bay
Delta National Wildlife Refuge
Shell Keys National Wildlife Refuge
Caillou Bay
Timbalier Bay
Terrebonne Bay
MISSISSIPPI RIVER DELTA
Pilottown

G U L F   O F   M E X I C O

miles
0   30

Interstate Highway
State Capital
Highest Point in the State
National Forest
National Historic Park
U.S. Highway
City or Town
Indian Reservation
State Forest
State Highway
Wildlife Refuge

G U L F   O F   M E X I C O

Map Skills

1. What mountain is west of Ruston?

2. To get from the state capital to Hammond, which interstate would you take?

3. What is the easternmost city or town on the map?

4. Which bay is south of Timbalier Bay?

5. Which state forest is south of Alexandria?

6. What river is east of the Bayou Cocodrie National Wildlife Refuge?

7. What direction does US Highway 171 run?

8. Which reservoir is on the state's western border?

9. Which city is north of Slidell?

10. What kind of waterway runs through Houma?

Answers

1. Driskill Mountain
2. I-12
3. Pilottown
4. Terrebonne Bay
5. Alexander State Forest
6. Mississippi River
7. North–south
8. Toledo Bend Reservoir
9. Bogalusa
10. Intracoastal Waterway

More Information

Books

Klar, Jeremy. *The Louisiana Purchase and Westward Expansion.*
New York: Rosen Publishing Group, 2016.

Richard, Zachary, Sylvain Godin, and Maurice Basque.
The History of the Acadians in Louisiana. Lafayette:
University of Louisiana at Lafayette Press, 2013.

Tracy, Kathleen. *Louisiana Creole and Cajun Cultures in Perspective.*
Newark, DE: Mitchell Lane Publishers, 2014.

Websites

Infographic: The Louisiana Purchase
https://www.kidsdiscover.com/infographics/infographic-louisiana-purchase
KIDS Discover presents an engaging look at the Louisiana Purchase.

Louisiana House Kids' Page
http://house.louisiana.gov/kids/default.htm
The Louisiana House of Representatives's website for
kids has fun facts about the state for students.

Louisiana: The Pelican State
https://kids.nationalgeographic.com/explore/states/louisiana
Explore pictures and interesting facts about Louisiana
on this site from National Geographic Kids.

Louisiana Tourism
http://www.louisianatravel.com
Louisiana's state tourism site provides information on
fun things to do in every region of Louisiana.

Index

Page numbers in **boldface** are illustrations. Entries in **boldface** are glossary terms.

African Americans, 23, 26, 31–32, 34–37, 40–41, 45–48, 50, 53–55, 57, 60, 66–67, 73–74
American Revolution, 27
Asian Americans, 48, 57

Baton Rouge, 4, 9–10, 12, **12**, 32–33, 36–38, 49, 54, 63, **68**, 70, **70**
bayous, **8**, 9–11, 14, 21, 46, 50, 55
Bridges, Ruby, 73–74, **74**

Cajuns (Acadians), 12, 27, 50, 52–55, **53**, 60
Civil War, 32–33, **33**, 50, 60
climate, 15, 18, 52, 59–60
Confederate monuments, 39, 42
Congo Square, 47, 66, **66**
corruption, 38, 41
crawfish, **6**, 18, 54–55, 60–61, **61**
Creole, 46–47, **46**, 52–54

dead zone, 19
delta, 11, 35
de Soto, Hernando, 4, 25
discernment, 17
diseases, 25–26, 45
dugout canoes, 24, **24**, 28

education, 32, 34, 37–38, **45**, 49–50, **49**, 64, **64**, 69–70, 73–74
Edwards, John Bel, 7, 69, **70**
endangered species, 11, 18, 21
estuary, 11

farming, 11, 18–19, 24, 26, 28–29, 32, 35, 37, 45, 47–48, 50, 59–60
festivals, 12, 55, 57, **57**
flooding, 10–11, 15, 36–38, **37**, **39**, 60
food, 7, 12, 24, 29, 43, **43**, 50–51, 54–55, **54**, 60–61
forests, 10, 13, 20, 61
French, 4–5, 16–17, 23, 25–28, 46–48, 50, 52–55
French and Indian War, 26–27

government
federal, 16–17, 27, 32, 34–37, 45–46, 73

local, 69, 72
state, 4, 7, 19, 31, 34–38, 41, **68**, 69–74, **70**
Great Depression, 36–37
Gulf of Mexico, 9, 11, 15, 18–19, **19**, 36, 62–63
gumbo, 7, 54–55, **54**

highest point, 10, **10**
Hispanic Americans, 48, 57
humidity, 15
hurricanes, 6, 15, **15**, 18, 38–39, **39**, 50, 57, 59

immigration, 26, 32, 45–48, 50, 52, 54
intimidation, 34–35
Isleños, 47, 55

Jackson, Andrew, 31–32, **31**
jazz, 23, 40–41, 47, 55–56, 66–67
Jefferson, Thomas, 16–17, **17**, 27

Katrina, Hurricane, 6, 18, 38–39, **39**, 50, 57, 59

Lafayette, 12, **12**, 49–50, **49**, 54, 61, 64
Lafitte, Jean, 31, **31**
lagniappe, 46
Lake Charles, 12, 38,

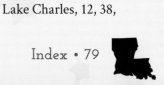